W9-CYV-707

The Amazon

River in a Rain Forest

By Molly Aloian

CRABTREE
Publishing Company
www.crabtreebooks.com

Crabtree Publishing Company
www.crabtreebooks.com

Author: Molly Aloian
Editor: Barbara Bakowski
Designer: Tammy West, Westgraphix LLC
Photo Researcher: Edward A. Thomas
Map Illustrator: Stefan Chabluk
Indexer: Nila Glikin
Project Coordinator: Kathy Middleton
Crabtree Editor: Adrianna Morganelli
Production Coordinator: Kenneth Wright
Prepress Technician: Kenneth Wright

Series Consultant: Michael E. Ritter, Ph.D., Professor
of Geography, University of Wisconsin—Stevens Point

Developed for Crabtree Publishing Company by RJF
Publishing LLC (www.RJFpublishing.com)

Photo Credits:
Cover: Medio Images/White/Photolibrary
4: © Yann Arthus-Bertrand/Corbis
6, 7, 8, 11 (top), 12: iStockphoto
11 (bottom): Nicole Duplaix/NationalGeographic/Getty
    Images
14: © Wolfgang Kaehler/Corbis
17: © Royal Geographical Society, London,
    UK/The Bridgeman Art Library
18: © Buddy Mays/Alamy
19: © BrazilPhotos.com/Alamy
20: © Paulo Fridman/Corbis
22: © Sylvia Cordaiy Photo Library Ltd./Alamy
23, 24: Luis Veiga/The Image Bank/Getty Images
25: AFP/Getty Images
27: © Peter Arnold, Inc./Alamy

Cover: Canoers on the Amazon River at the Breves Narrows
in Brazil.

Library and Archives Canada Cataloguing in Publication

Aloian, Molly
    The Amazon : river in a rain forest / Molly Aloian.

(Rivers around the world)
Includes index.
ISBN 978-0-7787-7442-6 (bound).--ISBN 978-0-7787-7465-5 (pbk.)

    1. Amazon River--Juvenile literature. 2. Amazon River Valley--
Juvenile
literature. I. Title. II. Series: Rivers around the world

F2546.A46 2010   j981'.1   C2009-906238-0

Library of Congress Cataloging-in-Publication Data

Aloian, Molly.
    The Amazon : river in a rain forest / by Molly Aloian.
        p. cm. -- (Rivers around the world)
    Includes index.
    ISBN 978-0-7787-7465-5 (pbk. : alk. paper) -- ISBN 978-0-7787-7442-6
(reinforced library binding : alk. paper)
    1. Amazon River--Juvenile literature. 2. Amazon River Valley--
Juvenile literature. I. Title. II. Series.

F2546.A42 2009
981'.1--dc22

                                                              2009042404

Crabtree Publishing Company
www.crabtreebooks.com   1-800-387-7650

Printed in the U.S.A./092015/CG20150812

Published in Canada
Crabtree Publishing
616 Welland Ave.
St. Catharines, ON
L2M 5V6

Published in the United States
Crabtree Publishing
PMB 59051
350 Fifth Avenue, 59th Floor
New York, New York 10118

Published in the
United Kingdom
Crabtree Publishing
Maritime House
Basin Road North,
Hove BN41 1WR

Published in Australia
Crabtree Publishing
3 Charles Street
Coburg North
VIC, 3058

CONTENTS

Words that are defined in the glossary are in **bold** type
the first time they appear in the text.

CHAPTER 1
The Amazing Amazon

The Amazon River is in the northern part of South America. It is the second-longest river in the world—about 4,000 miles (6,450 km) long. The farthest source of the Amazon River is high in the Andes Mountains of Peru. The river flows north and east across Brazil before emptying into the Atlantic Ocean. In terms of volume, the Amazon is the largest river in the world. It contains one-fifth of Earth's freshwater. A vast rain forest makes up more than two-thirds of the Amazon River's **drainage basin**.

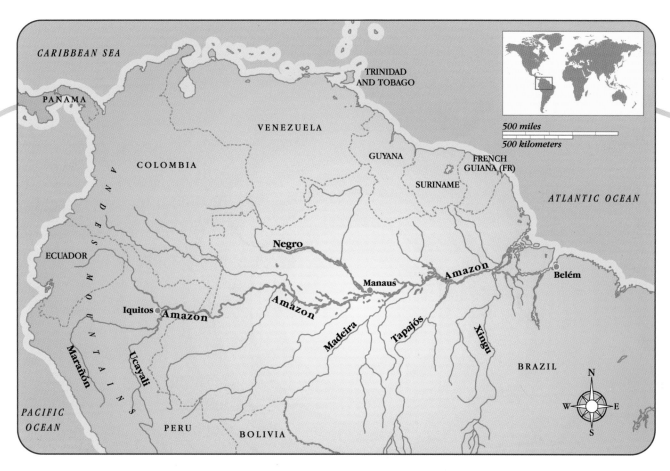

Many tributaries join the Amazon River as it flows eastward across South America.

Across a Continent

Melting snow from the mountaintops forms the Apurímac River, which flows down the Andes and joins the Ucayali River in east-central Peru. The Ucayali River meets the Marañón River near Iquitos, Peru. Where these two rivers come together, they form the Amazon River. Thousands of **tributaries** feed into the Amazon River along its course. The river system drains parts of Bolivia, Brazil, Colombia, Ecuador, French Guiana, Guyana, Peru, Suriname, and Venezuela. At its **mouth** on the northeastern coast of Brazil, the

LEFT: Because of its vast size, people sometimes refer to the Amazon River as a "river sea."

FAST FACT
The Amazon River is so wide that for much of its length it is impossible for a person standing on one bank to see the opposite bank.

5

The source of the Amazon River is high in the Andes Mountains of Peru.

in the region for at least 11,000 years. These people used the river as a source of drinking water, food, and transportation. The river enabled people to travel and to communicate with one another. It also helped separate the hunting and fishing grounds of different groups of **indigenous** people.

The arrival of Europeans in the 1500s brought many changes to the Amazon River basin. Although many Europeans came in search of gold and spices, they eventually set up **plantations** and began to use the natural resources of the forest. Trading posts and ports developed along the river so goods could be shipped back to Europe to be sold.

river separates into branches. The mouth of the main stream, the Pará, is about 50 miles (80 km) wide.

The Amazon River flows through the Amazon rain forest—the world's largest tropical rain forest. This **habitat** is rich in plant and animal life. The rain forest is made up of broad-leaved trees, flowering shrubs, and vines. It is home to millions of species of birds, monkeys, lizards, frogs, and other animals.

Relying on the River

People have lived in the Amazon River basin for thousands of years. Some **archaeologists** say humans have lived

A Modern View

The Amazon River is navigable for almost its entire length, so it is an important route through the continent. Today, modern port cities, such as Manaus in Brazil and Iquitos in Peru,

The Amazon River is an important means of travel for people who live in villages along the river.

lie along or near the river. Manaus is 900 miles (1,450 km) inland of the Atlantic Ocean. It has a population of about 1.4 million, making it the largest city in the river basin. More than 400,000 people live in the city of Iquitos. Small towns and native villages are scattered along the river, too. Because the forest is dense and crossed by a vast number of tributaries, some remote areas remain unexplored by humans.

The Amazon River is important to the region's **economy**. People log the hardwood forests within the Amazon River **floodplain**. Farmers grow food crops, such as sugarcane and soybeans, and raise livestock, including cattle, water buffalo, and goats, on land that has been cleared of trees. Other important economic activities include mining, trade, and tourism. Dams along the Amazon River tributaries produce **hydroelectricity**.

Human activities have threatened the region's **ecology**—and perhaps contributed to global weather and climate change. Logging, agriculture, and mining have contributed to **deforestation** and pollution. Growth of population and industry also endanger traditional ways of life of indigenous groups in the river basin.

What's in a Name?

The Amazon River basin is sometimes called Amazonia. It was given this name by the 16th-century Spanish explorer Francisco de Orellana. He was the first European to travel along the Amazon River. Orellana claimed to have fought with fierce groups of female warriors, similar to the Amazons of Greek mythology.

CHAPTER 2

On Course

The Amazon River basin contains a huge system of rivers. Thousands of small streams flow together to form larger rivers, which then flow into the mighty Amazon River. The river is so vast that it has been described as an "ocean of water" through a forest.

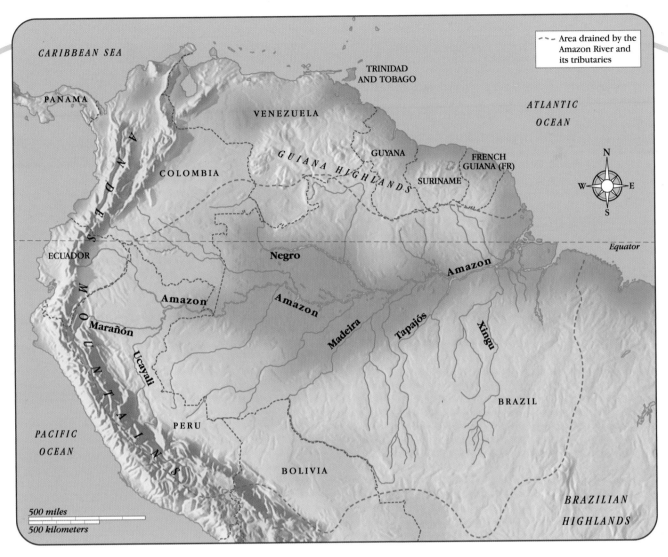

The Amazon River and its tributaries drain an area of more than 2.7 million square miles (seven million square km).

A Geologic History

According to **geologists**, the Amazon River originally flowed from east to west across the continent of South America. About 90 million years ago, two plates, or large movable sections that form part of Earth's shell, began to push into each other. This slowly created a massive uprising of land, eventually forming the Andes Mountains, which extend along almost all of the west coast of South America. As millions of years passed, a vast system of inland lakes and swamps formed. With the land now sloping downward from the Andes in the west

LEFT: The Amazon River is navigable for almost its entire length.

to the Atlantic Ocean in the east, the Amazon River cut its present course flowing east to the Atlantic.

The "River Sea"

Because of its vast size and power, some people describe the Amazon River as a "river sea." In just one hour, the Amazon River pours about 170 billion gallons (640 billion liters) of water into the Atlantic Ocean. The Amazon River has an unusually high number of tributaries. Some people estimate that number to be as high as 15,000. Its four main tributaries are the Negro River, the Madeira River, the Tapajós River, and the Xingu River. As the Amazon River flows east, these tributaries add water and **sediment**.

Small Stream Source

In 2000, a National Geographic Society expedition found that the most distant source of the Amazon River is a small stream on a mountain called Nevado Mismi. The mountain, in the Andes range in southern Peru, is more than 18,000 feet (5,486 m) high. The waters from the stream eventually flow into the Apurímac River, a tributary of the Ucayali River. The Ucayali River joins the Marañón River to form the Amazon River.

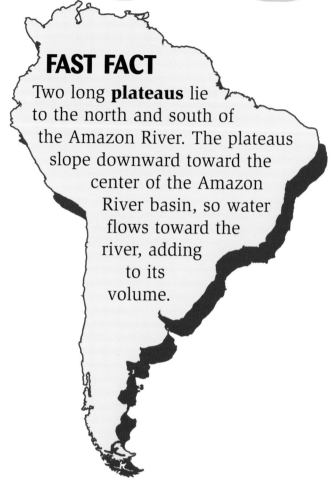

FAST FACT
Two long **plateaus** lie to the north and south of the Amazon River. The plateaus slope downward toward the center of the Amazon River basin, so water flows toward the river, adding to its volume.

Draining the Land

A **drainage pattern** is the arrangement of a main stream and its tributaries. The drainage pattern is determined by geologic features on and below the surface. The Amazon River has a **dendritic** drainage pattern, which looks like the branches of a tree. The Amazon River and its tributaries drain an area of more than 2.7 million square miles (seven million square km).

High Water

For part of the year, the banks of the Amazon River are flooded in many areas. Flooding occurs in different months in different places. Heavy rains

Lovely Lily

The Amazon water lily, the largest water lily in the world, grows in the Amazon River. Its huge leaves can grow to be seven feet (two m) across. Its flowers are about 12 inches (30 cm) across. Sugary sap collects at the base of the flowers and provides food for beetles and other insects.

Amazon water lilies are sometimes called water platters, a fitting nickname!

and melting snow from the Andes Mountains cause the volume of water in parts of the river to swell to about four times the usual volume. Land as far as 20 miles (32 km) on either side of the river can be covered in water. Some areas of forest can be under as much as 50 feet (15 m) of water for several months. Fish and reptiles take shelter and reproduce among the submerged tree trunks, branches, and leaves.

Unusually heavy rains can result in severe flooding, causing problems for people who live close to the river. Extensive flooding may force tens of thousands of people from their homes.

Amazon Plants

A wide variety of plant life makes up the Amazon rain forest, which covers much of the Amazon River basin. Some experts say about 80,000 known species of trees and 55,000 species

A giant river otter swims with a fresh-caught fish in its mouth.

Anaconda: River Giant

The anaconda can grow to be 20 feet (six m) long and can weigh up to 350 pounds (160 kg). This huge snake lurks at the edge of the Amazon River and feeds on tapirs, deer, fish, turtles, birds, and capybaras, which are large rodents that resemble guinea pigs. The anaconda coils itself around its prey, suffocating the animal. Then the anaconda swallows its victim whole, head first.

of flowering plants grow in the Amazon River basin. Half of these plants are found nowhere else on Earth. Trees such as teak, mahogany, chestnut, walnut, rosewood, and ebony are important natural resources.

The water hyacinth also lives in the Amazon River. This plant grows to be about three feet (one m) across. It has lush leaves and lavender-colored flowers. Its intertwining stems provide safe homes for newly hatched fish, called fry. The plant floats on the water, unattached to the river bottom. Its roots trail under water in a thick mat.

The slow-moving sloth rarely comes down from its home in the rainforest trees. The animal sleeps and eats while hanging upside down!

Amazon Animals

The Amazon River basin is home to an amazing variety of animals. A **canopy** of trees stretches above the floodplain, providing shelter for monkeys, macaws, harpy eagles, and dozens of species of lizards. Sloths hang from tree branches as they feed on leaves and shoots. The roars of howler monkeys can be heard at least two miles (3.2 km) away. Turtles, alligator-like animals called caimans, snakes, frogs, manatees, and fish live in the floodplain during the flood season. The pink Amazon river dolphin, also called the boto, swims among the trunks and branches of trees. The dolphin feeds on fish and crustaceans in the river. Giant river otters also eat fish and shellfish. They are some of the most endangered animals in the Amazon.

More than 8,000 species of insects live along the Amazon River. Thousands of brightly colored butterflies gather on riverside sandbanks. Green praying mantises rest on leaves, camouflaged from predators. Industrious leaf-cutter ants live in colonies containing millions of individuals. The ants spend their days gnawing off bits of leaves to take back to their nests. Black flies, wasps, and swarms of mosquitoes fill the humid air.

More than 1,500 known species of fish live in the waters of the Amazon

FAST FACT
Some people of the Amazon River basin use the jaws of the piranha as cutting tools and its teeth as razors.

River system. Scientists say many more fish species exist but have not been identified yet. Most of the fish species **migrate** to reproduce. Fish are an important food source for people who live in the Amazon River basin.

Piranhas are small fish with razor-sharp teeth. These fish are important to the Amazon River's **ecosystem**. They help keep fish populations strong and healthy by eating slower, weaker, or diseased fish. Piranhas also eat dead animals, helping get rid of flesh that would otherwise rot and pollute the waters of the Amazon River.

CHAPTER 3

Living in the Amazon

People have been living along the Amazon River and depending on it for their survival for thousands of years. The river provides them with food and water. Early Amazonian people were mainly hunters and gatherers, but some grew food crops in the fertile soil of the floodplains. By the middle of the 1500s, thousands of Spanish and Portuguese **missionaries**, explorers, and settlers had arrived in the Amazon River basin, where they set up sugar and tobacco plantations. Today, there are some large cities, such as Manaus and Belém in Brazil, with populations of more than one million.

Fishing and Hunting

Ancient Amazonian people used spears, **dip nets**, and hooks to catch fish from the river. They baited the hooks with worms, insects, and small fish. People boiled the fish in huge pots or smoked it to preserve it. Fish was an important part of their diet.

Men hunted birds, reptiles, and mammals that lived along the Amazon River and its tributaries. They used bows and arrows and tools called blowguns for hunting. A blowgun was a tube made from a hollow reed. Hunters placed a small, sharp piece of bone in the tube and blew a blast of air to shoot at their targets, such as birds or small monkeys. Women gathered wild grains, fruits, berries, and nuts.

Water for Crops

Some farmers who lived along the Amazon River reserved water from the floods. They built low earthen barriers to prevent some of the floodwaters from receding. This water was used to **irrigate** root crops, such as turnips, cassava, and yams, during dry periods. The water contained **silt**, which was rich in minerals and other nutrients

Coming Up for Air

The pirarucu, also called the arapaima, is one of the world's largest freshwater fish. It lives in the waters of the Amazon River. This giant fish can grow to be almost ten feet (three m) long and can weigh up to 485 pounds (220 kg). The pirarucu comes to the surface of the river to take in oxygen from the air, to supplement oxygen the fish takes in from the water through its gills. A pirarucu has a large tongue that is studded with teeth. Amazonian people caught the pirarucu for its meat and then dried the tongues and used them to grate seeds.

that helped crops grow well. This method of trapping water is known as basin irrigation. The trapped water would slowly soak down into the soil.

European Exploration

Europeans began traveling in and around the Amazon River in the 1500s. Francisco de Orellana, a Spanish soldier, explored the Amazon River from 1541 to 1542. He was on an

LEFT: The Jivaro, indigenous people of Brazil, hunt with blowguns and wear traditional clothing.

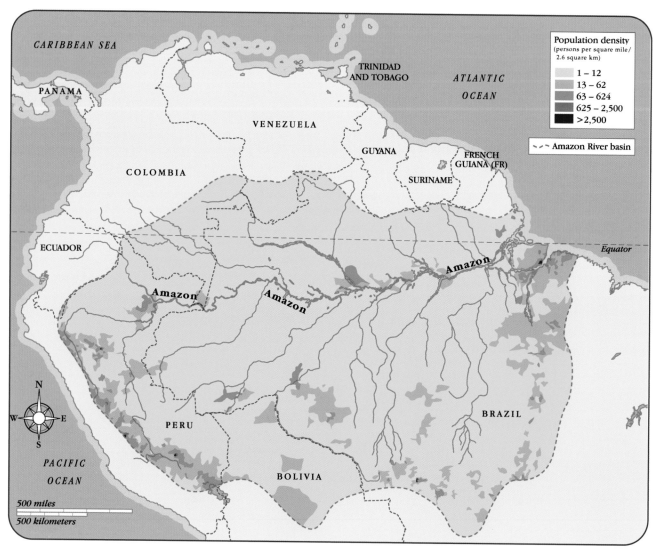

The population of the Amazon River basin is approximately ten million. People are mostly concentrated in cities along the river and its main tributaries.

NOTABLE QUOTE

"[The Amazon]…came on with such fury and with so great an onrush that it was a thing of much awe and amazement…. It was enough to fill one with the greatest fear just to look at it, let alone to go through it."

—Spanish missionary Gaspar de Carvajal

expedition commanded by Gonzalo Pizarro, who was in search of gold and spices. Orellana was ordered to sail down the Napo River with a crew to look for food and signs of treasure. He descended the Napo until it met the Amazon River, in present-day northeastern Peru. He did not find the gold and spices he sought. Instead of returning to Pizarro, however, Orellana and his men proceeded down the Amazon River to the Atlantic Ocean. The voyage to the coast lasted nearly eight months.

Over the next 50 years, European interest in the Amazon River continued to grow. Europeans were interested in logging the hardwood trees and harvesting the spices from spice trees. They realized that they could transport hardwoods and spices on the Amazon River. Spices such as cinnamon and clove, as well as cacao, were shipped to Europe to be sold. Cacao is produced from the dried seeds of an evergreen tree and is used to make chocolate and cocoa.

Diseases and Death

During the early 16th century, about seven million indigenous people lived in the Amazon River basin. The arrival

Naturalist Narrative

An English **naturalist** named Henry Walter Bates spent time along the Amazon River from 1848 to 1859. A naturalist is a person who studies animals, plants, and their habitats. Bates collected thousands of species of animals, particularly insects. He then wrote a book called *The Naturalist on the River Amazons*, in which he described his discoveries. Many people still consider Henry Walter Bates's book one of the most important books on the Amazon River.

Henry Walter Bates

of Europeans brought diseases that killed millions of indigenous people, reducing the native population by about 90 percent within a century. The native people had no immunity against diseases such as cholera and pneumonia.

Modern Life

Today, millions of people of different **ethnicities** live in the Amazon River basin. There are bustling cities and towns as well as remote villages along the river. Manaus and Belém, in Brazil, are large international ports. They boast beautiful buildings, large universities, and numerous restaurants and museums. However, some people are extremely poor and live in shacks on the edges of the cities. Iquitos, Peru, is a major port in the upper Amazon River region. The people who live on the outskirts of the city build their houses on stilts because of the seasonal flooding.

Manaus, Brazil, is the largest city in the Amazon River basin.

The Matis hunt with long blowguns, as their ancestors did long ago.

Today's Indigenous People

Today, some 500,000 indigenous people live in the Amazon River basin. Native groups include the Munduruku, the Yanomami, and the Matis. There may be as many as 75 other indigenous groups who choose to live in the Amazon rain forest without any outside contact.

The Munduruku live in villages in an area in the Brazilian state of Pará. They hunt, fish, and grow crops. The Yanomami people of Brazil and Venezuela live in large, circular communal houses that can hold hundreds of people. The central area is used for activities such as feasts and games. Matis hunters still use blowguns for hunting and are world-renowned for their skills with this tool. They hunt monkeys and other animals in the rainforest canopy.

In the villages scattered along the river, indigenous people still hunt, fish, and gather fruit. Some grow manioc, bananas, and beans on small plots of land.

CHAPTER 4
Travel and Commerce

The Amazon River has been a major transportation route since ancient times. The river helped the people living alongside it move from village to village and stay connected to each other. It also enabled them to transport and trade goods. Europeans used the river to ship spices and hardwoods back to Europe. Today, the river is still an important means of transportation and plays a key role in the region's economy.

Navigating the Amazon River

Historically, indigenous people traveled in small canoes and rafts. The most common craft was the dugout canoe, which is made by hollowing out a long log. Dugout canoes are heavy and sturdy. People made rafts from balsa logs, which are light and **buoyant**. People used the rafts to transport heavy loads.

Trees: An Amazon Treasure

During the second half of the 1900s, logging in the Amazon River basin increased to meet demand for hardwoods in Europe, Asia, and North America. Products made of teak, mahogany, chestnut, walnut, rosewood, and ebony were valued for the beauty of the wood, and the hardness of the wood also made such products strong and durable.

The timber industry still plays a huge role in the Amazon economy. Loggers cut down rainforest trees and then use the Amazon River to float the logs out of the forest. Oceangoing ships pick up the lumber and export it to other countries throughout the world.

LEFT: Logging is important to the economy of Amazon River basin countries, but deforestation is a serious problem.

FAST FACT
Amazonian people looking for gold were known locally as *garimpeiros*, which means "seeker of precious stones."

Rubber Boom

Rubber trees were plentiful in the Amazon floodplain. During the 1830s, Europeans developed many uses for rubber, including waterproofing shoes and clothes. From the 1890s through the 1920s, rubber from the Amazon River basin was in high demand for bicycle and automobile tires used around the world.

In the 1860s, approximately 3,000 tons (2,700 metric tons) of rubber was being exported annually from the Amazon basin. By 1911, annual rubber exports had grown to about 44,000 tons (39,900 metric tons). Hundreds of thousands of native Amazonian people worked as rubber tappers, removing the sap from trees. They were not paid fairly; some were even forced to work as slaves for "rubber barons," who became extremely wealthy from the rubber trade.

The Amazon rubber boom did not last, however. By the 1920s, rubber was being produced more cheaply in other parts of the world. As a result, rubber could be purchased for cheaper prices. Hundreds of thousands of Amazonian rubber tappers and their families were plunged into poverty.

Gold Strike

Gold was discovered throughout the Amazon River basin in the late 1960s and early 1970s. Local Amazonian people rushed to the Amazon River and its many tributaries because these waters were the largest source of gold in the river basin. By the 1980s, gold was the most important export from the Amazon River basin. Between $2 billion and $3 billion worth of gold was being exported from the region each year to countries all over the world. Today, more than a million prospectors pan for gold in the Amazon River in Brazil and Venezuela.

Mining in the Amazon

Oil and minerals, such as **bauxite** and iron ore, lie under the ground in the Amazon River basin. Oil is pumped out of the ground in Ecuador and Peru. A pipeline in Ecuador moves oil over the Andes Mountains to oil **refineries** on the Pacific coast. The Grande Carajas project in Brazil is a major center for mining iron ore. The Carajas mine is the largest iron ore mine in the world.

Agriculture

Farmers grow crops, including oil palms, soybeans, bananas, beans, and sugarcane, on land that has been cleared. Brazil is the leading producer of

Hoping to strike it rich, prospectors pan for gold in an Amazon River tributary.

Setting Up Ranches

By the 1980s, many huge cattle ranches had been set up on land that was already cleared by logging in Brazil, Bolivia, and Venezuela. Some of the beef is eaten locally, but much of the meat is exported.

soybeans in South America. Rice and corn (maize) are major crops on small plantations. Cacao, Brazil nuts, coffee, and other crops are also grown. Most of this produce is exported to other countries.

Gone Fishing

Fishing is an important economic activity in the Amazon region. Some people still fish in traditional ways, but others work on large **trawlers**.

Thousands of people work at transporting the fish and selling it in markets throughout the Amazon region. Many species of fish sell for high prices because they are rare or difficult to catch.

Hydroelectric Power

The water of the Amazon River and its tributaries is used to create hydroelectricity for people living within the river basin. Large cities have plenty of electricity. Power lines are even going up in some remote villages. Two of the largest dams within the Amazon River system are on the Itaipu and Tucurui rivers.

Touring the Amazon

Tourism is also important to the Amazon's economy. Tourists spend money on lodging, food, and locally produced goods. Tour companies offer boat trips through parts of the Amazon River and the rain forest. Visitors can see the region's plants and wildlife—from giant water lilies to giant river otters—in their natural habitats.

Harvesting coffee beans in Brazil.

CHAPTER 5

An Amazon at Risk?

Today, many factors threaten the Amazon River and the entire river basin. Deforestation, **overfishing**, and dam-building are just some of the activities that are harming the rainforest ecosystem. However, many individuals and environmental organizations are working to protect the Amazon River basin and the wide variety of plants, animals, and people living within it.

Deforestation

One of the most serious problems in the Amazon River basin is the destruction of the rain forest. Mining, logging, and the clearing of land for farms, roads, and ranches destroys the habitats of thousands of plant and animal species that live in the rain forest and in the region's rivers. When trees are removed from an area, birds, monkeys, snakes, and other tree-dwelling animals lose their habitats.

Deforestation contributes to the erosion, or washing away, of soil during the rainy season. Because trees are no longer anchoring the soil, mudslides occur.

Deforestation is also an important factor in global **climate change**. By taking in carbon dioxide through their leaves and storing carbon, trees can reduce the amount of carbon dioxide in the atmosphere. When people clear areas of forest land, there are fewer trees to take carbon dioxide from the air. Also, when forest land is cleared by burning the trees, carbon stored in the wood returns to the atmosphere and combines with oxygen to form carbon dioxide. Carbon dioxide and other **greenhouse gases** trap the Sun's heat close to Earth, contributing to a gradual rise in the average temperature in Earth's atmosphere.

Fighting for the Rain Forest

Chico Mendes was born into a poor family in 1944 and grew up in the Amazon rain forest. He worked as a rubber tapper and organized a union called the National Council of Rubber Tappers. Mendes and the union worked to stop loggers and ranchers from clearing large parts of the rain forest. They persuaded the Brazilian government to reserve small areas of land for **sustainable** uses, such as rubber tapping. Some people opposed Mendes and his work in defense of the rain forest and its people. Ranchers murdered Mendes in 1988.

LEFT: Cattle ranching is bringing about deforestation in the rain forest. Much of the cleared land is used to graze livestock.

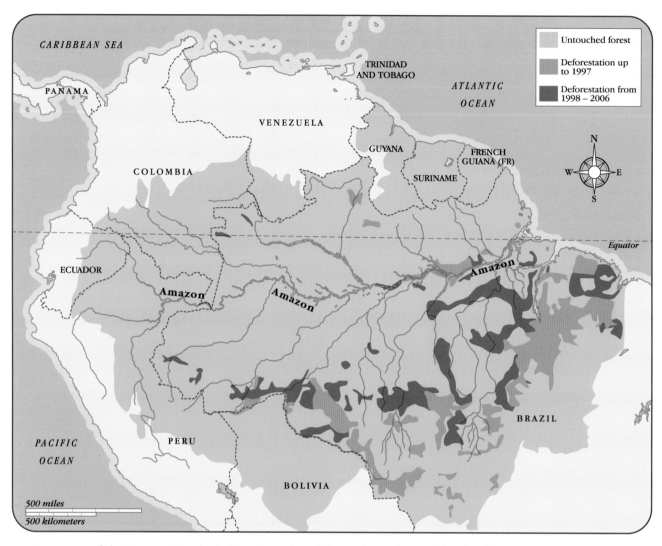

Large areas of the Amazon River basin have been cleared for cattle ranches and farmland.

Overfishing

Overfishing is another major threat to many species. Since the 1970s, fish populations in the Amazon River have dropped steadily. Fishers are now catching a greater number of young fish. Because these fish will not grow to maturity and reproduce, some species may be at risk of becoming endangered.

NOTABLE QUOTE

"The development we want is based on the concept of "good living," which encompasses our health, clean water, a healthy environment, and a strong culture."

—Ines Shiguango, president, Confederation of Indigenous Nations of the Ecuadorian Amazon

Dam Damage

Although dams have dramatically increased the supply of electricity along the Amazon River, they have damaged the basin's ecology. The building of dams and the creation of reservoirs within the Amazon River system has caused flooding in the surrounding land. It has destroyed large areas of forest that provided a habitat for thousands of plants and animals and displaced many people.

By blocking the natural flow of water, dams prevent nutrient-rich silt from reaching the floodplain and nourishing the forest. Dams have also disrupted the migration routes of fish. The fish can no longer migrate to their spawning grounds, causing fish populations to decrease each year.

Mercury Pollution

Mercury pollution is a serious problem in the Amazon River and its tributaries. Mercury is a silver-white poisonous metallic liquid. In the process of extracting gold, miners flush poisonous mercury into the water. As fish eat microorganisms in the water, the mercury enters the food chain and poisons many other animals. People who eat mercury-contaminated fish may become sick and die.

Saving the Amazon

Environmental organizations are working to save areas of the Amazon River basin. Some logging companies are no longer cutting down huge areas of forest. Loggers remove only a few trees in each square mile of forest. Government agencies are acting to protect fish stocks. Cleaner gold-mining technologies are being developed, too.

Many indigenous people of the Amazon River basin are campaigning to keep their traditional lands and to protect them from destruction by loggers, cattle ranchers, and other commercial operations. Indigenous groups are also working to protect the waters where fish spawn. They encourage commercial fishing companies to stop overfishing.

Dams on the river system supply needed electricity but also damage the environment.

COMPARING THE WORLD'S RIVERS

River	Continent	Source	Outflow	Approximate Length in miles (kilometers)	Area of Drainage Basin in square miles (square kilometers)
Amazon	South America	Andes Mountains, Peru	Atlantic Ocean	4,000 (6,450)	2.7 million (7 million)
Euphrates	Asia	Murat and Kara Su rivers, Turkey	Persian Gulf	1,740 (2,800)	171,430 (444,000)
Ganges	Asia	Himalayas, India	Bay of Bengal	1,560 (2,510)	400,000 (1 million)
Mississippi	North America	Lake Itasca, Minnesota	Gulf of Mexico	2,350 (3,780)	1.2 million (3.1 million)
Nile	Africa	Streams flowing into Lake Victoria, East Africa	Mediterranean Sea	4,145 (6,670)	1.3 million (3.3 million)
Rhine	Europe	Alps, Switzerland	North Sea	865 (1,390)	65,600 (170,000)
St. Lawrence	North America	Lake Ontario, Canada and United States	Gulf of St. Lawrence	744 (1,190)	502,000 (1.3 million)
Tigris	Asia	Lake Hazar, Taurus Mountains, Turkey	Persian Gulf	1,180 (1,900)	43,000 (111,000)
Yangtze	Asia	Damqu River, Tanggula Mountains, China	East China Sea	3,915 (6,300)	690,000 (1.8 million)

TIMELINE

About 150 million years ago	The Amazon River begins to form.
About 90 million years ago	The Andes Mountains begin to form in western South America, changing the slope of the land. The Amazon River begins to flow toward the east.
3000 BC	The first known large human settlements in the Amazon River basin are established.
300–1300 BC	At least 100,000 people live on an island in the Amazon River delta.
1500 AD	Vicente Yáñez Pinzón sails about 60 miles (96 km) up the soon-to-be-named Amazon River.
1541–1542	Francisco de Orellana is the first European to travel the length of the Amazon River.
Mid-1500s–1700	Europeans force large numbers of Amazonian native people into slavery.
1848–1859	English naturalist Henry Walter Bates studies animals (mostly insects) of the Amazon region.
1860	Annual rubber exports in the Amazon River basin reach about 3,000 tons (2,700 metric tons).
1930s	The "rubber boom" in the Amazon basin ends.
1988	Chico Mendes, a rubber tapper, union leader, and conservationist in Brazil, is killed.
Early 1990s	The indigenous population of the Amazon River basin is about 600,000.
2000	Scientists find the small stream in the Andes Mountains of Peru that is believed to be the source of the Amazon River.
Early 2000s	The indigenous population of the Amazon River basin drops to about 200,000.

GLOSSARY

archaeologists Scientists who study the material remains (such as fossils and artifacts) of past human life and activities

bauxite A claylike substance that is the main ore of aluminum

buoyant Capable of floating

canopy The uppermost layer of vegetation in a forest

climate change A change in the typical weather a place experiences over time

deforestation The action or process of clearing an area of trees and underbrush

dendritic Branching like a tree

dip nets Small nets used to scoop fish

drainage basin The area of land drained by a river and its tributaries

drainage pattern The arrangement of a main stream and its tributaries

ecology The relationship between living and nonliving things and their environment

economy The way money and goods are produced, distributed, and consumed

ecosystem A complex community of organisms and their environments functioning as a unit

ethnicities Classifications of people according to common racial, national, tribal, religious, linguistic, or cultural origin or background

floodplain The flat land along a river that is covered by water during a flood

geologists Scientists who study the history of Earth and its life, especially as recorded in rocks

greenhouse gases Gases that contribute to the trapping of the Sun's heat within Earth's atmosphere, linked to a gradual rise in average temperatures worldwide

habitat The environment in which a plant or an animal naturally lives and grows

hydroelectricity Electricity that is produced by using the movement of water

indigenous Living or occurring naturally in a certain region or environment

irrigate To water land in an artificial way to foster plant growth

migrate To move periodically from one region to another for feeding or breeding

missionaries People who are sent to spread a religious faith in a territory or foreign country

mouth The place where a river enters a larger body of water

naturalist A person who studies animals, plants, and their habitats

overfishing The depletion of fish populations below an acceptable level by extensive fishing

plantations Large farms on which crops are grown, often by resident workers

plateaus Broad, flat areas of high land

refineries Buildings where metals, oil, or sugar are refined

sediment Material deposited by water, wind, or glaciers

silt Small particles of sand or rock left as sediment

sustainable Describing activities or methods than can be kept up because they do not deplete or harm natural resources

trawlers Boats used for fishing with large nets dragged below the surface of an ocean, sea, lake, or river

tributaries Smaller rivers and streams that flow into larger bodies of water

FIND OUT MORE

BOOKS

Reynolds, Jan. *Amazon Basin*. Lee and Low Books, 2007.

Schoones, Simon. *The Amazon*. Hodder Wayland Children's, 2005.

Thompson, Gare. *Amazon Journey: Cruising the Rain Forest*.
    National Geographic Children's Books, 2006.

Ylvisaker, Anne. *The Amazon River*. Compass Point Books, 2005.

Zronik, John. *Francisco Pizzaro: Journey through Peru and South America*.
    Crabtree Publishing Company, 2005.

WEB SITES

TheAmazon.org
www.theamazon.org

Eduweb: Amazon Interactive
www.eduweb.com/amazon.html

Extreme Science: Amazon River
www.extremescience.com/AmazonRiver.htm

World Wildlife Fund: Amazon
www.worldwildlife.org/what/wherewework/amazon/index.html

ABOUT THE AUTHOR

Molly Aloian has written more than 50 nonfiction books for children on a wide variety of topics, including endangered animals, animal life cycles, continents and their geography, holidays around the world, and chemistry. When she is not busy writing, she enjoys traveling, hiking, and cooking.

INDEX

Page references in **bold** type are to illustrations.